GUILTY, GUILTY, GUILTY!

In this **Doonesbury** volume, Marvelous Mark Slackmeyer's endearing ravings go entirely unabridged. His WBBY Watergate broadcasts, which caused such consternation among the nation's newspaper editors, herein are happily published along with Pat Nixon's testimony to the Ervin Committee, Ron Zeigler's alleged press briefings, Superstar Jeb Magruder's smash lecture tour, and inevitably, R. M. "Dick" Nixon's Operation Candor. And for those who have wearied of wallowing, GUILTY, GUILTY, GUILTY! has other surprises: Yuri Yetsky, Russian man of letters; Skip Willis, POW in a time-warp; and Zonker Harris, mailperson and screener of bad tidings.

THE DOONESBURY PHENOMENON

In less than five years, a remarkable new comic strip called **Doonesbury** has provoked more public and media reaction than any cartoon in the last twenty years, winning legions of loyal followers and becoming the first comic strip awarded the Pulitzer Prize. Michael J. Doonesbury and the denizens of Walden commune appear in nearly four hundred newspapers with a readership of over 23 million.

Bantam Books by G. B. Trudeau

CALL ME WHEN YOU FIND AMERICA
GUILTY, GUILTY, GUILTY!

Guilty, Guilty, Guilty!

A Doonesbury Book · by G. B. Trudeau

BANTAM BOOKS
TORONTO NEW YORK LONDON

To Annie, of course

RL 7, IL 8-up

GUILTY, GUILTY, GUILTY!

*A Bantam Book / published by arrangement with
Holt, Rinehart and Winston*

PRINTING HISTORY

Holt, Rinehart and Winston edition / June 1974
2nd printing . . . . August 1974   3rd printing . . . . April 1975
Bantam edition / March 1976
2nd printing . . . . April 1976   3rd printing . . . . December 1977
4th printing . . . . . August 1979

ISBN 0-553-13288-1

Published simultaneously in the United States and Canada

PRINTED IN THE UNITED STATES OF AMERICA

0 9 8 7 6 5 4

1

ARE THERE ANY MORE QUESTIONS?

MR. YETSKY, IS IT TRUE YOU WERE ONCE SELF-EFFACING?

DA. I CONFESS THAT WHEN I CAME TO THIS COUNTRY YEARS AGO, MY SPIRIT WAS LACKING IN CONFIDENCE. BUT ONE FALL DAY, AS I DROVE THROUGH MICHIGAN TO A READING IN DETROIT, I WAS BLESSED WITH A VISION!

MY GENIUS CAME TO ME IN A REVELATION! "YETSKY," I SAID, "IT'S TRUE, COMRADE — YOU ARE INDEED THE EXTRAORDINARY MORTAL! YOU ARE... TRUTH!"

WHEN I REACHED DETROIT, I BOUGHT MY SHADES.

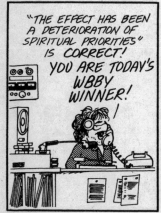

MIKE, IT'S INCREDIBLE HOW MANY PEOPLE WHO COME IN HERE ARE TALKING ABOUT MARK'S NEW RADIO SHOW...

I SAW "MARVELOUS" HIMSELF ON THE STREET YESTERDAY. HE TOLD ME HE'S BEEN ENJOYING EVERY MINUTE OF IT...

REALLY?

WELL, ACTUALLY, THERE IS THE PROBLEM OF THE ADS...

THE ADS?

..AND SOAKS UP EXCESS SKIN OIL! TOUGH AGAINST BLACKHEADS, TOO!

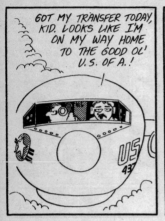

GIVE THE UNIVERSITY A SMALL CHECK? NO, SIR, NOT I! I HAVE NOTED WITH GREAT ALARM YOUR RADICAL APPROACH TO EDUCATION, AND I REFUSE TO SUPPORT IT!

OH, WELL, I GUESS THAT'S THE WAY IT GOES... SAY, I UNDERSTAND YOU HAVE A SON APPLYING FOR ADMISSION NEXT FALL.

HE'LL GET A NICE ROOM, WON'T HE?

I CAN'T PROMISE YOU ANYTHING.

47

SAY, SKIP, HAVE YOU MET BERNIE YET?

NO. MIKE TOLD ME ABOUT HIM, THOUGH. HE'S INTERESTED IN SCIENCES, RIGHT?

THAT'S RIGHT. HE SPECIALIZES IN WHAT HE CALLS "MOLECULAR TRANSFORMATION."

HE'S ALWAYS TURNING HIMSELF INTO WEIRD CREATURES — LAST YEAR IT WAS WEREWOLVES, BUT THIS YEAR HE AND MIKE ARE TESTING SOME NEW VARIATIONS.

O.K., NOW WHAT?

BREATHE IN. DEEPER.

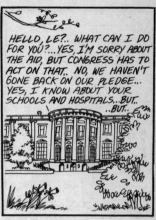

NICHOLE, HAVE YOU HEARD ABOUT MARK'S NEW SERIES OF PROFILES ON HIS RADIO SHOW?

NO. WHAT'S IT ON?

THE WATERGATE CONSPIRATORS. HE'S WORKED OUT COMPLETE BIOGRAPHIES ON ALL OF THEM.

BOY, I'LL BET THEY'RE JUST **BRUTAL!**

NOT AT ALL. I READ THEM LAST NIGHT. SOME OF THEM ARE QUITE SENSITIVE.

"LOS ANGELES IS A LONELY TOWN TO GROW UP IN, ESPECIALLY IF YOU'RE A SMALL BOY NAMED H. R. HALDEMAN."

"UPON YOUR EXIT FROM THE **HO CHI MINH** TRAIL, TURN LEFT ONTO THE SCENIC MOUNTAIN PATH WHICH TRAVERSES THE HIGH COUNTRYSIDE.

"IF THE FERRY OVER THE MEANDERING **MEKONG** ISN'T WORKING, YOU MAY HAVE TO GET YOUR FEET WET. BE SURE TO BRING ALONG SOME DRY, LIGHTWEIGHT SUMMER CLOTHES FOR WHEN YOU REACH THE OTHER SIDE.

"A QUICK SCRAMBLE UP THE BEAUTIFUL **DINO-LINO** CLIFF FORMATION AND YOU SHOULD BE ABLE TO SPOT A SMALL LEDGE 80 YARDS ABOVE YOU. A SHORT, SPIRITED HIKE, AND THE TOURIST WILL SOON FIND HIMSELF AT THE TOP.

"WELCOME TO LAOS."

GBTrudeau

DAVID, YOUR RECENT BOOK, "THE BEST AND THE BRIGHTEST" HAS REALLY TAKEN OFF! HOW DO YOU EXPLAIN IT?

I THINK, MERV, THAT THE QUESTIONS OF THE VIETNAM QUAGMIRE HAVE LED MANY PEOPLE TO BECOME CURIOUS ABOUT THESE BRILLIANT JOHNSON AND KENNEDY AIDES WHO FIRST GOT US INVOLVED OVER THERE.

WELL, I WOULD THINK THAT WOULD BODE WELL FOR YOUR NEXT BOOK, DAVID. AS I UNDERSTAND IT, RECENT EVENTS HAVE INSPIRED YOU TO START WORK ON A HOT NEW SEQUEL!

THAT'S RIGHT, MERV. IT'S CALLED "THE WORST AND THE STUPIDEST."

OH? WHAT'S IT ABOUT?

WE INTERRUPT THE SENATE WATERGATE HEARINGS TO BRING YOU THIS SPECIAL BULLETIN.

TODAY ON THE PRE-EMPTED SOAP OPERA, "AS THE HOSPITAL TURNS," DR. HARDIN FINALLY DECIDED TO DIVORCE HIS WIFE RACHEL, AFTER FIVE YEARS OF MARRIAGE! A BITTER CUSTODY FIGHT IS EXPECTED.

TO REPEAT: DR. HARDIN IS GETTING A DIVORCE FROM RACHEL! THAT'S A FINAL.

WE NOW RETURN TO OUR REGULARLY SCHEDULED BROADCAST.

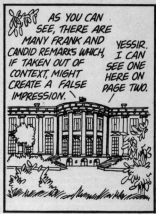

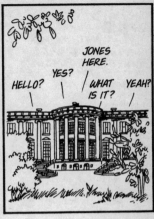

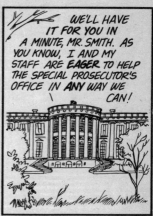